7/09

W9-CCM-998

3 2186 00163 9391

GARETH STEVENS
VITAL SCIENCE
Earth Science

EARTH'S CORE AND CRUST

by Barbara J. Davis
Science curriculum consultant: Suzy Gazlay, M.A.,
science curriculum resource teacher

GARETH**STEVENS**
PUBLISHING
A Member of the WRC Media Family of Companies

Fossil Ridge Public Library District
Braidwood, IL 60408

Please visit our web site at: www.garethstevens.com
For a free color catalog describing Gareth Stevens Publishing's
list of high-quality books and multimedia programs, call
1-800-542-2595 (USA) or 1-800-387-3178 (Canada).
Gareth Stevens Publishing's fax: (414) 332-3567.

Library of Congress Cataloging-in-Publication Data

Davis, Barbara J.
    Earth's core and crust / Barbara J. Davis.
        p. cm. — (Gareth Stevens vital science - earth science)
    Includes bibliographical references and index.
    ISBN-13: 978-0-8368-7762-5 (lib. bdg.)
    ISBN-13: 978-0-8368-7873-8 (softcover)
    1. Earth—Core—Juvenile literature.   2. Earth—Crust—Juvenile literature.
    3. Geodynamics—Juvenile literature.   I. Title.
    QE509.2.D38   2007
    551.1—dc22   2006033115

This edition first published in 2007 by
Gareth Stevens Publishing
A Member of the WRC Media Family of Companies
330 West Olive Street, Suite 100
Milwaukee, WI 53212 USA

This edition copyright © 2007 by Gareth Stevens, Inc.

Produced by White-Thomson Publishing Ltd.
Editor: Brian Fitzgerald
Designer: Clare Nicholas
Photo researcher/commissioning editor: Stephen White-Thomson
Gareth Stevens editorial direction: Mark Sachner
Gareth Stevens editor: Leifa Butrick
Gareth Stevens art direction: Tammy West
Gareth Stevens production: Jessica Yanke and Robert Kraus

Science curriculum consultant: Tom Lough, Ph.D., Associate Professor of Science Education, Murray State
University, Murray, Kentucky

Illustrations by Peter Bull Art Studio
Photo credits: CORBIS, pp. 16 (© Jonathan Blair), 17 (© Gerald Favre/Geologos), 31 (© Lloyd Cluff), 33
(© David Butow/CORBIS SABA), 34 (© T.MUGHAL/epa), 35, 36 (Bettmann), 37 (© Arno Balzarini/epa),
38 (© Choo Youn-Kong/Pool/Reuters), 44 (© Yann Arthus-Bertrand); Geoscience, pp. 25, 39, 42t;
©iStockphoto.com, pp. 8 (Mike Morley), 9 (both; inset Stephan Hoerold), 10 (Geoff Kuchera), 12
(Matthew Cole), 19 (Beth Whitcomb), title page and 27 (Chris Crafter), 29 (Irina Efremova), 42b (Bill
Gruber), 45l and br (Sascha Burkard), 45tr (Natalia Bratslavsky); NASA, p. 4; TopFoto.co.uk, p. 9; U.S.
Geological Survey, p. 11 (J.D. Griggs); Woods Hole Oceanographic Institution, pp. 6, 23 (both; inset Rod
Catanach).

Cover: Molten rock and gases escape through Earth's crust at volcanoes—often with spectacular results.
Kilauea on Hawaii is one of the most active volcanoes on Earth.
Title page: The Great Rift Valley in Africa formed when two tectonic plates pulled apart from each other.

All rights reserved. No part of this book may be reproduced, stored in a retrieval system, or transmitted in
any form or by any means, electronic, mechanical, photocopying, recording, or otherwise, without the prior
written permission of the copyright holder.

Printed in Canada

1 2 3 4 5 6 7 8 9 10 10 09 08 07 06

TABLE OF CONTENTS

1 INTRODUCTION

A system is something that has components, or parts, that come together to form a whole. A bicycle is a type of system. It has a number of parts, such as gears, chains, and wheels, that work together to allow the bicycle to move. Earth is also a system. It has countless parts that work together to allow our planet to support life.

One major part of Earth's system is the geosphere. The prefix *geo-* is from a Greek word for "earth," as in "ground or land." The geosphere is the solid surface on which you stand. The land surface might be a rocky bluff or a level farm field. It can be a cave located deep underground or the highest of mountains. The solid surface might also be the ocean floor and all the valleys, mountains, and ridges located there. Whether the solid surface is out your back door or at the bottom of the ocean, it is the part of Earth's geosphere called the crust.

The word *crust* brings up images of an object sitting on top of or surrounding another object. Piecrust surrounds sweet pie filling. Bread crust is the thin, top layer that surrounds the soft inner loaf. Earth's crust also surrounds or sits on top of something else.

Under Earth's crust, molten rock, gases, and water do a slow dance. These materials surround the hot, solid center of Earth called the core. Earth's core and crust usually interact with each other in very subtle ways. We do not notice most of the steps of the slow dance that is taking place miles beneath our feet.

▼ Earth's geosphere includes the solid surface that forms the ocean floor, as well as the land on which people live.

Sometimes, however, the interaction between Earth's core and crust can produce dramatic results. Huge landmasses slowly move and bump into each other, causing giant rocks to fold in on themselves or to crack. Such movement might trigger the massive shaking of an earthquake. Pressure builds and explodes through a weakened part of Earth's crust, perhaps through a volcano that spews rivers of molten rock and tons of hot ash. In many cases, such events lead to widespread destruction and loss of life. Can these events be predicted ahead of time? What do we need to know?

This book about Earth's core and crust is intended to answer those questions. Many mysteries about what goes on in Earth's hidden layers remain to be solved. Geologists—scientists who study Earth— are learning more and more about how processes taking place far below Earth's surface affect us all.

We do not have the ability to prevent an earthquake or a volcanic eruption. We do, however, have the power to better understand Earth. This understanding helps us live with the mysteries for which we have answers, as well as with the mysteries whose answers we still seek.

▼ Volcanic eruptions, such as the June 1991 explosion of Mount Pinatubo in the Philippines, are stunning evidence of the intense pressure and heat that lie below Earth's surface.

2 EARTH'S LAYERS

If you could cut a big wedge out of Earth, you would see that our planet is made up of layers. The major layers are called the crust, mantle, outer core, and inner core. The layers differ in thickness, chemical properties, and physical characteristics. They also interact with and affect each other in several ways.

The Crust

The crust is Earth's outer layer and also its thinnest. The crust is about 25 miles (40 kilometers) at its thickest point. If a person were trying to tunnel through the crust, 25 miles would be quite a distance. The distance from Earth's crust to the center of its core, however, is almost 4,000 miles (6,430 km). Compared with 4,000 miles, 25 miles is not so deep. In fact, the relative thickness of the crust to the rest of Earth is something like the thickness of an onion's skin to the rest of its layers. Earth's crust contains a number of different materials, including oxygen, aluminum, iron, calcium, sodium, silicon, potassium, and magnesium.

Two types of crust are found on Earth. The continental crust lies under all the continents and large landmasses. Landforms such as mountains, canyons, and even some types of caves sit on the continental crust. Continental crust is made up mostly of rocks, such as granite. Although it contains crystals of other substances, granite is basically cooled material from beneath the crust.

The oceanic crust forms the ocean floor. More than two-thirds of Earth's

▲ The ocean floor is made up of volcanic lava that seeped through cracks in the crust and hardened into solid rock.

surface lies beneath oceans, so there is far more oceanic crust than continental crust. Oceanic crust is made up mostly of a volcanic rock called basalt. Basalt is denser than granite.

It is easy to think that a denser rock means a thicker rock, but that is not the case. Density is the mass, or weight, of a substance that exists in a particular volume. If you held a 1-inch (2.5-centimeter) cube of basalt in one hand and a 1-inch (2.5-cm) cube of granite in the other, the basalt would be heavier.

The oceanic crust is thinner than the continental crust. At some points, the ocean floor is only about 3 miles (5 km) thick. Just how thin is that? At a quick pace, a person could walk about 4 miles (6.4 km) in an hour!

The Lithosphere

If it were possible for scientists to tunnel completely through Earth's crust, they would eventually cross into the next major layer, the mantle. Unlike the rest of the mantle, the uppermost part is cold

Earth's Layers

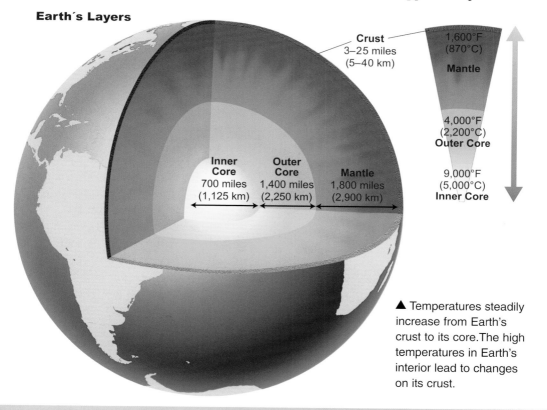

Crust	3–25 miles	(5–40 km)
	1,600°F	(870°C)
	Mantle	
	4,000°F	(2,200°C)
	Outer Core	
	9,000°F	(5,000°C)
	Inner Core	

Inner Core	Outer Core	Mantle
700 miles (1,125 km)	1,400 miles (2,250 km)	1,800 miles (2,900 km)

▲ Temperatures steadily increase from Earth's crust to its core. The high temperatures in Earth's interior lead to changes on its crust.

▲ The basalt columns of Giant's Causeway in Northern Ireland were caused by volcanic eruptions more than 60 million years ago.

and pressure increase closer to the center of Earth.

The temperature in the top part of the crust would be somewhat cool—probably pretty close to the air or water temperatures where the scientists began their journey. About 66 feet (20 meters) down, the lithosphere starts to get warmer. At this point, the temperature increases about 34° Fahrenheit (1° Celsius) every 132 feet (40 m). The temperature continues to rise at this rate for several miles. The rate of increase in temperature slows down but continues through the lithosphere, finally reaching almost 1,600°F (870°C).

and rigid. The crust and the upper mantle together form the lithosphere. *Lithos* is the Greek word for "stone." The lithosphere is a stiff, stony layer that includes all the continents and the ocean floor. The average thickness of the lithosphere is about 62 miles (100 km).

If the scientists traveled down through the lithosphere, their instruments would show that the temperature was getting warmer. They would also notice that the pressure was becoming greater. This is because, in general, both temperature

Journey to the Center of the Earth?

One of the deepest mines in the world is in South Africa. It is a gold mine that tunnels 2.17 miles (3.5 km) below the surface of Earth. It takes miners ten minutes in a fast elevator to reach the bottom of the deepest mine shaft. A person standing at the bottom of that mine would be surrounded by solid rock—Earth's crust. It would be easy to feel as if the whole Earth were pressing in on all sides. Even at that depth, though, the mine is little more than a scratch on Earth's continental crust.

▲ Vesuvius in Italy may look like an ordinary mountain from a distance, but it is actually one of the world's most active volcanoes. *(Inset)* The lava that constantly flows from Hawaii's Kilauea volcano gives clues about Earth's interior. The surface of the island is made of hardened lava.

The Mantle

Earth's next main layer, the mantle, is also its thickest. This rocky layer extends about 1,800 miles (2,900 km) into the planet—almost halfway to the center of Earth. The mantle is made up of oxygen, iron, silicon, and magnesium. The chemical makeup does not change much throughout the mantle, but temperature and pressure increase dramatically deeper into Earth's interior.

The temperature in the top areas of the mantle reaches almost 1,600°F. By comparison, water at sea level boils at 212°F (100°C). Pizzas bake in what is considered a "hot" oven at 425°F (218°C). At almost four times the temperature of a pizza oven, 1,600°F is hot enough to melt some types of rocks.

Melting rock is exactly what the scientists would see as they passed through the area where the stiff structure of the lithosphere gives way to the asthenosphere. This layer is about 110 miles (180 km) thick. The intense heat in the asthenosphere makes the material soft enough to flow very slowly. Picture something like hot candle wax. The lithosphere actually floats on the softened, slow-moving asthenosphere.

Deeper into the mantle, the pressure increases, and the mantle material below the asthenosphere becomes denser. Scientists estimate that about 235 miles (380 km) into the mantle, the pressure is 110,000 times greater than the air pressure at Earth's surface. By 435 miles (700 km) in, the pressure is about 250,000 times greater than it is on the surface. The temperature in the mantle also increases drastically, rising from 1,600°F in its uppermost layers to almost 4,000°F (2,200°C) closer to the core.

The Outer Core

Earth's core is actually two separate areas, the outer core and the inner core. At almost 4,000°F, Earth's outer core is hot enough to melt more than rocks. This liquid layer is made up mainly of two melted metals, iron and nickel.

Although the pressure in the outer core is extremely high, the intense heat keeps this layer in a liquid state. Like all liquids, the molten material in the outer core moves. This movement is probably something like the currents in rivers.

The outer core is the second thickest of Earth's layers. It is almost 1,400 miles (2,250 km) from the uppermost part of the outer core to the beginning of Earth's last main layer, the inner core.

The Inner Core

Like the outer core, the inner core is made up mostly of iron and nickel. Unlike the outer core, however, the inner core is a dense, solid metal sphere. The

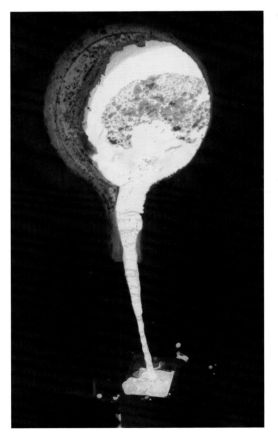

▲ Molten iron is poured into a mold at a foundry. Most of Earth's outer core is made up of this dense molten mineral.

The Core Specialists

Study of the Earth's Deep Interior (SEDI) is an international scientific group that focuses its studies mainly on Earth's core and mantle. The group's goal is to help people better understand how Earth's interior formed and how the planet's present characteristics affect processes and structures on its crust. SEDI currently has more than 500 members, including chemists, geologists, volcano specialists, physicists, and other scientists who are interested in unraveling the mysteries hidden deep beneath Earth's crust.

▶ Volcano experts sometimes get very close to the action. Here, a geologist takes measurements near the erupting Kilauea volcano.

inner core is solid because pressure there reaches 45 million pounds per square inch (3.16 million kilograms per square centimeter)—3 million times the air pressure you would feel if you were standing at sea level. It is hard to imagine pressure that high, but if you were standing in Earth's inner core, there would be enough pressure to compress you into an object smaller than a marble!

The solid state of the inner core is even more amazing when you consider that its temperature is estimated to be greater than 9,000°F (5,000°C). So Earth's inner core is almost as hot as the Sun! Although the inner core is certainly hot enough to melt metal, the enormous pressure squeezes the iron and nickel atoms to such an extent that they cannot spread out and change to a liquid state.

Scientists believe that Earth's core got much of its heat at the time the planet was formed. Even after 4.5 billion years, the core has not cooled off. Additional heat comes from the breakdown of radioactive materials, such as uranium, thorium, and potassium, that are present in Earth's core.

Earth's Magnetic Field

Earth's inner core is not only extremely hot, it also spins. The currents in the liquid outer core are strong enough to cause the dense inner core to revolve. The inner core revolves slightly faster than the rest of Earth. The combination of motion and the core's metal makeup creates a magnetic field. This invisible field turns Earth into a giant bar magnet. Lines of force in this magnetic field affect all parts of the planet, including the crust.

Like a bar magnet, Earth has magnetic poles. A compass points to the north

▲ The poles on a bar magnet function in the same way that Earth's magnetic poles do. The iron filings in this photo show the outline of the magnetic field that surrounds the magnet.

Measuring Magnetism

The amount of magnetism on Earth varies from place to place. One reason is that different types of rock have different degrees of magnetism. Rocks that contain iron are more magnetic than others. Scientists use an instrument called a magnetometer to detect magnetism and measure how much of it is present in an area or an object. Magnetometers are used in satellite surveys of Earth. They also valuable tools for hunting for ship-wrecks or other buried items of historical value. Magnetometers also help geologists locate needed iron deposits.

pole—Earth's magnetic north pole, not the exact geographic location of the northernmost point on the planet. Earth's magnetic field is constantly changing, so the locations of its magnetic poles change, too.

Heat Transfer and Earth's Inner Core

Heat transfer is the movement of energy from a warmer object or substance to a cooler one. The immense heat at Earth's core transfers out through a process called convection. Convection is the transfer of heat by the movement of heated fluid—a liquid or gas.

Heating a liquid or gas causes the particles to move faster. As they move faster, the particles also spread farther apart. A greater distance between particles means less density in the fluid. If the temperature of the fluid decreases, the particles slow down and tend to move closer together. As a result, the fluid's density increases.

Have you ever heated a pot of soup on a stove? As the soup at the bottom of the

Convection Currents

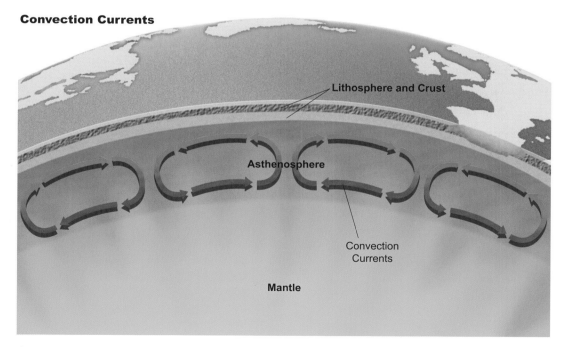

▲ The transfer of heat from Earth's core to its crust takes place in the asthenosphere. Warmer, less dense mantle material rises to the top of the asthenosphere. At the same time, cooler, denser mantle material drops to the bottom. The constant exchange of material creates convection currents.

pot starts to heat up, its particles move faster, spread out, and become less dense. Because it is less dense, the warming soup travels toward the surface, where it floats over the cooler soup. As the warmer soup at the surface cools, however, it becomes denser. Gravity pulls the denser soup toward the bottom of the pot, where the heating process begins again. Soon there is a constant flow of warm soup rising and cooler soup sinking. This flow of heat from one part of a fluid to another is called a convection current.

As described above, the changes in temperature and density in a fluid along with the force of gravity set convection currents in motion. In the example, the fluid is soup broth. Within Earth, the fluid is hot mantle material. The heat in the mantle comes from Earth' core.

The substances that make up mantle material have different densities. High temperatures cause some of the less dense mantle material to rise toward the top of the asthenosphere. As this material cools, it sinks back down into the lower part of the asthenosphere. This continuous rising and sinking of hot fluid creates a convection current under the lithosphere and crust. The convection current transfers some of the heat from Earth's core and mantle up through the remaining layers.

Mapping Earth's Layers

How do geologists know that the lithosphere is more solid than the mantle or that the inner core is solid metal? Although a trip to Earth's core may sound exciting, no vehicle could tunnel that far. Instead, geologists infer certain things about the materials that make up the inner Earth based on characteristics for which they can get real measurements.

Most of the discoveries scientists have made about the makeup of Earth's layers have come from measuring seismic waves caused by earthquakes. The seismic waves that travel through Earth's interior are called body waves. These waves of energy travel in all directions and bounce off the materials that are part of Earth's interior.

The way in which a seismic wave bounces off molten material is different from the way it bounces off solid rock. Some materials pass seismic waves along; others, such as liquids, absorb them. Scientists can determine how much of a material is solid and how much is liquid by the way the seismic waves travel through the material. By carefully studying the behavior of waves, scientists were able to conclude that Earth's outer core is liquid and that its denser inner core is solid.

③ DRIFTING CONTINENTS

In 1915, a German meteorologist named Alfred Wegener started a lot of discussion and arguments in the scientific community when he published his book *The Origin of Continents and Oceans.* In the book, Wegener suggested that the continents of Europe, Africa, and North and South America were once connected. He named this huge landmass Pangaea, meaning "all lands." He believed that about 200 million years ago, Pangaea began to break apart. Separate landmasses formed and eventually became the continents that we know today. He called his theory continental drift.

At the time, Wegener's idea seemed ridiculous to most scientists. All the continents were connected, and then they just split apart and drifted away from each other? Nonsense, they said! What force could possibly be strong enough to pull continents apart? Wegener did not have the technology to prove his theory, but he did provide some very good evidence to support his ideas.

Continental Drift

225 Million Years Ago

65 Million Years Ago

Present

▲ Over the course of about 225 million years, Earth's single landmass split apart, and the continents slowly drifted to their current spots.

This evidence was found by studying fossils, climate change over time, and the landforms themselves.

Fossils in Strange Places

A fossil is a preserved sign, or proof, of past life. A fossil might be an impression left in soft rock by an animal's bones or the leaves of a plant. A fossil might also be parts of the animal or plant itself, such as the teeth of a dinosaur.

Wegener found that fossils of certain animals and plants were present in continents very far away from each other. For example, the fossils of a plant called *Glossopteris* were discovered in South America, Africa, India, Australia, and Antarctica. This plant's seeds were too heavy to be carried by wind across oceans. The seeds were also too fragile to float through miles and miles of seawater. Birds could not have carried the seeds, because they had not yet evolved at the time *Glossopteris* lived, about 300 million years ago.

Fossils of prehistoric reptiles were also found on those continents. Like modern reptiles, those creatures were cold-blooded. They could not regulate their body temperatures as mammals do. Because of this, an environment in which the temperature was constantly frigid

▲ This fossil of the prehistoric reptile *Lystrosaurus* was discovered in Africa. Fossils of the same creature have been found as far away as Antarctica—evidence that the two continents were once connected.

would be a dangerous place for reptiles. Imagine how a lizard would react to life in the frozen climate of Antarctica today!

So how did *Glossopteris* and the reptile fossils end up on so many continents? According to Wegener, the fossils are evidence that there used to be one huge landmass on Earth. The fossils are also evidence that the weather in some of today's very cold places was a whole lot warmer at one time.

Climate Conflict

Spitsbergen is an island in the Arctic Ocean that lies north of the Scandinavian country of Norway. If you enjoy very cold temperatures and a lot of ice, you would find Spitsbergen to your liking. One

thing you would not expect to find there, however, would be a tropical plant. Surprisingly, that is exactly what Wegener discovered—fossils of tropical plants on Spitsbergen.

Other scientists of Wegener's day claimed that Earth's climate must have drastically changed over time. Wegener disagreed. He offered the Spitsbergen tropical plants as evidence that the island was, at one time, part of a larger land-mass located closer to the equator.

Wegener presented other evidence to support his theory that the positions of the continents have changed. He pointed out that the unique marks left by glaciers

▼ This glacial cave in Iceland shows scratches caused by the glacier's movement over rocks.

could be found in some odd places. A glacier is a huge mass of ice that can form over thousands of square miles of land. When glaciers move over rocks, they leave distinctive types of deep scratches. The presence of these scratches is one of the things geologists and climatologists use to determine what Earth's climate was like millions of years ago. Wegener observed that evidence of glaciers could be found on continents where today there is rarely a snowflake, much less ice. The southern portions of Africa, South America, and Australia all have rock formations with these telltale glacier scratches.

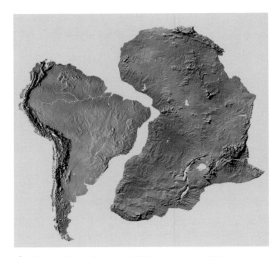

▲ South America and Africa look as if they could easily fit together. Wegener offered this as proof that the two continents were once part of a single landmass.

Puzzling Landforms

To support his theory of continental drift, Wegener offered as evidence the shapes of the continents themselves. The next time you look at a world map, try to imagine the continents tucked into each other like pieces of a jigsaw puzzle. Look closely at the east coast of South America and certain parts of the west coast of Africa. It seems as if the two continents might have been joined at one time. Take away the land that is Central America and it looks as though the northern coast of South America could fit into the southern part of North America where the Gulf of Mexico exists today. India might fit into

the eastern coast of Africa. Even Antarctica and Australia look as if they might have been connected.

Of course, Wegener went further than the idea of a big jigsaw puzzle. He presented evidence that certain mountain ranges on different continents appeared to have been a part of the same range. For example, a part of the Appalachian Mountains in North America seems to cut off abruptly at the coast of the Atlantic Ocean. Across the ocean, the Caledonian Mountains of Great Britain appear to do the same thing. When these "ends" are brought together, as Wegener suggested, they seem to fit as if both

▲ At one time, the Appalachian Mountains were connected to the Caledonian Mountains in Great Britain, on the other side of the Atlantic Ocean.

ranges were once part of one longer mountain range.

Wegener also observed distinctive mineral formations with the same chemical and physical compositions on landmasses thousands of miles apart. Coalfields in North America seem to line up with similar coalfields in some European countries, for example.

What Caused the Continents to Drift?

Even though Wegener had a great deal of strong evidence, scientists rejected his theory. Wegener did not have an answer to the key question: What force caused Pangaea to break apart? He also could not explain what caused huge landmasses to float to new locations. Think about the power needed to move a large

ship across the ocean. What would it take to move an entire continent?

Wegener believed that continental drift was partly due to a gravitational pull toward Earth's equator. In his day, however, there was no method available to prove this or any similar theory. So Wegener's ideas remained only a strange theory until the early 1960s. At that time, new discoveries led scientists to look once more at his ideas.

Geophysicists

How did Earth evolve? What is its internal structure? What causes earthquakes? Is Earth's magnetic field changing? These are a few of the many questions geophysicists try to answer. These scientists look at electronic data that measures Earth's magnetism at different places and times around the planet. They use the energy waves created by earthquakes to learn more about one of Earth's most dramatic physical events. Some geophysicists study ancient fossils and landforms to learn more about the changes Earth has gone through over millions of years. Marine geophysicists take their studies to the deepest part of the ocean—the oceanic crust and beyond. To become a geophysicist, you need to know a lot about subjects such as math, earth science, and computers.

4 SPREADING SEAFLOORS

Some of the proof that Wegener needed but could not find was at the bottom of the ocean. It was hidden thousands of feet down in areas where scientists had been unable to explore. When scientists began to map the ocean floor in the 1960s, they were astonished at what they found.

If you asked most people to name the longest chain of mountains on Earth, they would likely say the Himalayas in Asia, the Rocky Mountains in North America, or some other famous range. Surprisingly, the longest mountain chain on Earth is located deep in the ocean. Known as the mid-ocean ridge, it extends into all the world's major oceans.

The mid-ocean ridge is 40,000 miles (64,000 km) long and encircles Earth in an irregular pattern. The ridge has mountains, canyons, and other formations like those found on Earth's continental crust. Parts of the ridge are named for the regions where they are found. For example, the Mid-Atlantic Ridge runs through the central Atlantic Ocean. In fact, the ridge appears to split the ocean into two almost equal parts. Some of its peaks rise 10,000 feet (3,000 m) above the ocean floor. They are about as high as many of the peaks in the Rocky Mountains. The island of Iceland, in the North Atlantic Ocean, is part of the mid-ocean ridge. Most of the mid-ocean ridge formations, however, are far below the surface of the sea.

Great Global Rift

We have all seen a picture of the Grand Canyon in Arizona. In places, this natural wonder is more than 1 mile (1.6 km) deep. Now imagine a canyon more than twice as deep as the Grand Canyon. This underwater canyon is called the Great Global Rift, and it runs the entire length of the mid-ocean ridge.

Movement on the Ocean Floor

The mid-ocean ridge and the global rift were important discoveries that led scientists to ask more questions. How did the ridge and rift form? Did either of them

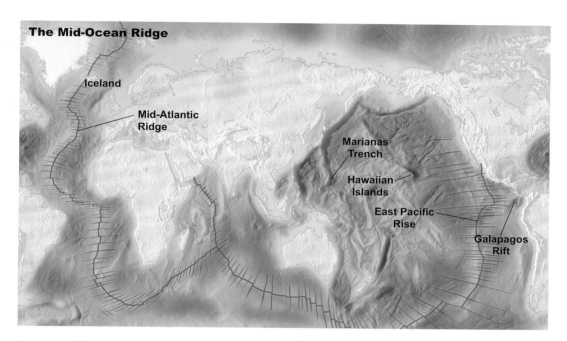

The Mid-Ocean Ridge

Iceland

Mid-Atlantic Ridge

Marianas Trench

Hawaiian Islands

East Pacific Rise

Galapagos Rift

have anything to do with the movement of the continents?

In 1960, American geologist Harry Hess came up with a startling idea. He proposed that the ocean floor slowly and continuously changes. It does this through the action of the mantle just under the oceanic crust. Molten mantle material rises and pushes through cracks in the oceanic crust. These cracks are located around the mid-ocean ridges and rifts. As the molten material pushes up through a crack, it moves older ocean floor to either side of the ridge. When the hot mantle material cools, it expands and forms a strip of new, rocky ocean

▲ The mid-ocean ridge snakes between the continents and through all the world's oceans.

floor. This activity is repeated when more hot mantle material flows up through the crack, once again spreading out and pushing aside the existing rock. In this way, new material is continually added to the ocean floor. Hess called this process seafloor spreading.

By the 1960s, science technology had come a very long way from Wegener's day. Researchers now had the ability to collect the evidence Hess needed to back up his theory. Beginning in 1968, a deep-sea drillship called the *Glomar Challenger* cut rock samples from the ocean floor. At times, the ship worked in water nearly 4 miles deep—more than sixteen times the length of the Empire State Building! Its drill cut columns of rock, called cores, that were 30 feet (9 m) long. Each core contained samples of the rock layers through which the drill had bored. When scientists tested the samples, they found that the oldest rocks had been found in areas farthest from the mid-ocean ridge.

Ocean-Floor Deep Drilling

The drillship *Glomar Challenger* was retired in 1985. It was replaced by an even more technologically advanced scientific drillship called the *JOIDES Resolution*. JOIDES stands for Joint Oceanographic Institutions for Deep Earth Sampling. Since 1985, more than 200 expeditions have taken place aboard the *JOIDES Resolution*. During an expedition in 2005, drillers dug nearly 1 mile (1.6 km) into the seafloor.

A Japanese drillship called *Chikyu* (meaning "Earth") plans to drill almost 5 miles (8 km) into the ocean floor in late 2006. Scientists hope to collect the first samples ever taken from Earth's mantle. The ocean-floor samples collected by drillships such as the *JOIDES Resolution* and *Chikyu* will provide scientists with the data they need to learn more about the formation and structure of Earth's layers.

The newest rocks were found closest to the center of the ridge. This discovery showed that seafloor spreading had taken place, as Hess believed.

Other expeditions during the 1960s allowed scientists to get a firsthand look at some of the seafloor. Using a small, square submersible vehicle called *Alvin*, researchers observed odd, pillow-shaped rocks. These types of rocks form only when molten mantle material quickly hardens after coming into contact with cold water. The rocks were evidence that mantle material had been regularly coming through cracks in the ridge.

Further observations revealed patterns in the seafloor rocks. Because the rocks are actually cooled molten mantle material, they contain iron. As the molten material cooled, the pieces of iron lined up like tiny compass needles set in the direction of Earth's magnetic poles. It was as if Earth had made its own magnetic memory chip.

When scientists tested the seafloor rocks, they found that the magnetism in the rocks formed an alternating "striped" pattern. One stripe had the normal magnetism. In the next stripe, the poles had been reversed. Reversed poles would cause the needle on a compass to point south instead of north. The next stripe over, the magnetism was normal once

Alvin's Deep-Sea Adventures

In the early 1960s, the U.S. Navy and the Woods Hole Oceanographic Institution (WHOI) in Massachusetts developed the submersible *Alvin (above)*. The deep-sea diving vehicle was unlike anything the world had ever seen. Named for WHOI scientist Allyn Vine, the craft holds three crew members in an area that is only 6 feet (1.8 m) in diameter. Although its passengers are cramped, *Alvin* has helped scientists see things they never dreamed existed. In 1975, *Alvin* took scientists down a bone-crushing 12,000 feet (3,650 m) to get a direct view of seafloor spreading along the Mid-Atlantic Ridge. In 1977, a dive into the Galapagos Rift near Ecuador offered the first look at geothermal vents and the never-before-seen animals that live there—including giant tube worms *(above, inset)*. In four decades of service, *Alvin* made more than 4,000 dives. A new version of *Alvin* is set to launch in 2008. This higher-tech submersible will be able to dive more than 21,325 feet (6,500 m). At that depth, scientists will be able to explore more than 99 percent of the seafloor.

again, and so on through the remaining stripes. This pattern showed that Earth had reversed its magnetic poles at different times during the planet's history.

Deep-Ocean Trenches and Subduction

New seafloor, or oceanic crust, is created at different rates depending on the location of the ridge. For example, between Europe and North America, about 2.2 inches (5.6 cm) of seafloor is added each year. In another area, called the East Pacific Rise, 12.6 inches (32 cm) of ocean floor is created every year! Even at a rate of only a few inches added each year, it would seem that the ocean floor would continue to grow wider and wider. Earth is not expanding like an over-inflated balloon, however, so where does all the "old" ocean floor go after it is pushed away?

Even though the seafloor spreads, it also sometimes slides down into gigantic underwater canyons called deep-ocean trenches. The deepest ocean trench lies 6.78 miles (11 km) below sea level in the North Pacific Ocean. Known as the Marianas Trench, it is the deepest location of Earth's oceanic crust.

Such trenches form in areas where Earth's oceanic crust bends downward. These areas are located closer to the outer edges of the ocean, where the

Shrinking (and Expanding) Oceans

The Pacific Ocean is ringed with many deep trenches where a lot of subduction takes place. More oceanic crust is lost to subduction than the mid-ocean ridges can produce. The result? The Pacific Ocean is shrinking!

The Atlantic Ocean, however, is expanding. The Atlantic does not have the Pacific's deep trenches, so there is no place for spreading seafloor to go. Also, the oceanic crust of the Atlantic Ocean is joined to the continental crust of the landmasses that surround the ocean. As the oceanic crust moves, it also pushes on the continental crust, moving it at the same rate. The result is that the oceanic crust gets a bit larger—and so does the Atlantic Ocean.

oceanic crust and the continental crust come together. Here, a process called subduction takes place.

During subduction, gravity pulls the older seafloor beneath a deep-ocean trench and then down into Earth's mantle. Seafloor spreading and subduction act like a giant conveyor belt that moves the seafloor out from the mid-ocean ridge. It takes millions of years for the ocean floor to be totally renewed through subduction and seafloor spreading.

Geothermal Vents

There is no light in the deepest parts of the ocean. In many deep ocean areas, temperatures are only 32°F to 37.5°F (0°C to 3°C). Such cold and dark conditions do not encourage life. In the deepest parts of the ocean, however, live some of Earth's most unusual creatures. These creatures live where the water temperature is much warmer, often more than 200°F (93°C). How can there be so much heat surrounded by so much cold? The answer lies in cracks in the ocean floor called geothermal vents.

Vents are cracks in the oceanic crust that allow molten material or gas to escape. Ocean water sinks through these cracks and comes into contact with material from Earth's mantle. When the ocean water contacts the hot mantle material, the water shoots back into the ocean. The water around geothermal vents is much warmer because the mantle material is about 1,800°F (1,000°C). These hot bursts of water mix with the cold ocean water. The water around the vents then becomes warm enough to support some very interesting life-forms.

◀ Geothermal vents on the ocean floor look like chimneys shooting out black smoke.

5 PLATE TECTONICS

Slowly, evidence was building in support of Wegener's original idea of continental drift. For the first time, scientists were gaining a true understanding of how seafloor spreading and subduction at deep-ocean trenches changed the landscape of Earth's crust. In 1965, Canadian geophysicist J. Tuzo Wilson put forth a theory that would provide the final missing piece in the puzzle of how continents could drift. It would also explain why Earth's crust remains a very active place. The new geological theory was called plate tectonics.

If you were to take a hard-boiled egg and tap it on a counter, the shell would crack in an uneven pattern. Earth's lithosphere can be compared to that cracked eggshell. The theory of plate tectonics proposes that the lithosphere is broken up into a series of uneven "plates" separated by relatively thin cracks. Plates consist of parts of both continental and oceanic crusts. The plates float on the asthenosphere, where convection currents help transfer heat from deep inside

Earth. These currents under the plates cause the plates to be in constant motion.

The plates are fitted together so tightly that any movement in one plate affects all the other plates around it. They may push up against each other, slide past each other, or pull apart. It may sound as if the plates bounce off each other like giant pinballs, but their movement is extremely slow. Tectonic plates move at a rate of 1 to 4 inches (2.5 to 10 cm) per year. This is about the rate at which your fingernails grow. This slow movement may not seem very exciting, but over millions of years it has caused dramatic results on Earth's surface. These results include deep-ocean trenches, earthquakes, volcanoes, and mountains.

Plate Boundaries

The edges where the plates meet are called plate boundaries. These boundaries extend deep into Earth—about 125 miles (200 km) in some places. There are three types of plate boundaries—divergent, convergent, and transform.

A divergent boundary is one where two plates move apart. The word *diverge* means "to separate and go in different directions." Many divergent boundaries are found at the mid-ocean ridge.

Divergent boundaries are also found on land. When two land plates pull apart, a very deep valley, called a rift valley, can form. The Great Rift Valley in eastern Africa formed more than 30 million years ago. Its divergent plate boundaries are still slowly moving apart. Some geologists believe that the rift may someday completely separate the eastern part of Africa from the rest of the continent. As

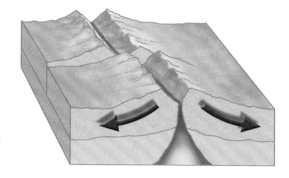

▲ At a divergent boundary, two plates move apart. This movement allows molten material from the mantle to rise to the surface. When the material cools, it forms a new layer of crust.

▼ Hell's Gate National Park in Kenya lies on the floor of the Great Rift Valley.

the rift widens, the valley floor drops. It may someday drop so far that it will be filled with seawater.

A convergent boundary is the opposite of a divergent boundary. Instead of two plates pulling apart, a convergent boundary is where the plates meet. The word *converge* means "to come together."

When two automobiles meet at the same point, they collide. When two enormous tectonic plates come together, there is also a collision. Remember, however, that the plates are traveling very slowly.

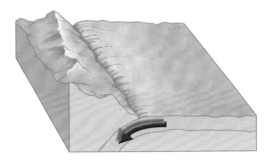

▲ At a convergent boundary, one plate often slides under another. Here, an oceanic plate meets a continental plate. Subduction occurs as the denser oceanic plate slips down toward the mantle. The result is a deep-ocean trench.

What happens during the collision depends on which types of plates are involved. It can take millions of years for the results of the collision to form.

Continental plates can converge with other continental plates or with oceanic plates. In the same way, two oceanic plates can converge. When two plates of any type converge, the denser plate will slide or drop beneath the other. Earlier you learned that continental crust is less dense than oceanic crust. If a continental plate and an oceanic plate converge, the oceanic plate is pushed under the continental plate and sinks. In other words, subduction takes place, forming deep-ocean trenches.

Oceanic crust becomes denser as it moves away from the mid-ocean ridge. Therefore, when two oceanic plates meet at a deep-ocean trench, the older, denser plate will push under the lighter one, slide down into the trench, and eventually return to the mantle. The long, narrow area where one plate slides under another is called the subduction zone.

Continental plates are not dense enough to push each other downward. Instead, the plates push on each other with enormous force. The continental crust is squeezed together and rises, forming mountains. About 50 million years ago, the continental plate that carries modern India began converging with the plate that carries Asia. The result was the Himalayas. This range is the home of the world's fourteen highest peaks, including the highest, Mount Everest.

▲ The Himalayas are the impressive result of a collision of two continental plates.

The third type of plate boundary is a transform boundary. At a transform boundary, two plates moving in opposite directions slide past each other. The plates can move side to side or up and down. At first glance, it might not seem as if this kind of movement would really change much on Earth's crust. There is no pulling apart to form oceans or valleys, as with divergent boundaries. The plates do not push up against each other with great force to make mountains, as with convergent boundaries. Like all plate boundaries, however, a transform boundary is uneven. When these two uneven surfaces scrape past each other,

there is sure to be grinding, breaking, shaking, and more. Just how much of this activity takes place depends largely upon something called a fault.

▼ At a transform boundary, two plates slide past each other. This movement creates neither mountains nor valleys. Instead, it may cause an earthquake.

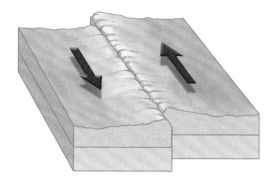

29

6 EARTHQUAKES

Faults are breaks in Earth's crust where huge blocks, or slabs, of the crust slide past each other. Faults are created by the force of the tectonic plates squeezing and pulling on the uppermost layer of Earth's crust. Over millions of years, this constant force causes the rocky crust to break. When the crust breaks, the rocks on either side of the break shift position in relation to one another. This shift causes some friction.

Friction describes the force between two surfaces rubbing together. The more uneven the surfaces, the greater the friction will be. Friction builds up as the edges of a fault slide against each other. If the edges of the fault are fairly smooth, the plates will slide by each other without the rocks sticking together too much. If the edges of the fault are very rough, however, it is possible that the edges will get stuck. When the edges finally release and slide past each other, they will do so with a great amount of force.

Have you ever pushed really hard on a jammed door only to have it suddenly swing wide open? If so, you probably fell through the doorway. While you were pushing on the door, you were storing up energy that was translated into motion as soon as the force you were pushing against went away. Likewise, the more the rocky sides of a transform fault stick or wedge against each other, the more energy is stored. When the sides quickly release, there is a big jolt. Then the sides leap past each other before returning to their normal speed of movement. That jolt is an earthquake.

Because faults are usually found along Earth's plate boundaries, that is where most earthquakes occur. In fact, if you research the locations of most earthquakes over the last few centuries, you will see that they define the boundaries of Earth's tectonic plates.

In North America, there is a transform boundary between the North American Plate and the Pacific Plate. This boundary is the location of the San Andreas Fault. The fault is really a series of faults that is almost 800 miles (1,290 km) long. The San Andreas Fault runs from the Salton Sea in Southern California, up most of the California coast, and into the Pacific Ocean. The fault is not only long but also deep. It extends at least 10 miles (16 km) into the ground. In addition to being long and deep, the San Andreas Fault has several areas where friction is quite high. A long, deep fault with many friction spots is likely to generate some pretty strong earthquakes. The fact that the San Andreas Fault also runs under the major cities of Los Angeles and San Francisco is cause for real concern.

▲ The San Andreas Fault marks the boundary between the North American and Pacific Plates.

The Myth of Losing California

There is a long-standing story that someday an enormous earthquake along the San Andreas Fault will shake some of the state of California loose and send it drifting into the Pacific Ocean. Although the threat of a massive earthquake in the region is real, the rest of the story is pure science fiction.

The hard facts, however, might be even more exciting. Along the San Andreas Fault, the two plates are slipping past each other on a horizontal course—very slowly. One day, San Francisco and Los Angeles will be directly across from each other instead of almost 400 miles (640 km) apart. Of course, since the plates are slipping past each other at a rate of only 2 inches (5 cm) per year, this shift won't be completed for a while—about another 15 million years!

Differences in Earthquakes

There are about 500,000 earthquakes each year that are strong enough to be measured in some way. Of these, 100,000 can be felt on the surface, yet only about 100 cause damage. It may sound as if earthquakes are not as dangerous as people think they are. Although it is true that not all earthquakes result in heavy damage, some are deadly. So what is the difference between a "mild" earthquake and a "severe" earthquake?

When friction builds up, the pressure eventually causes the rock along the fault line to break apart. The result is a release of stored energy in the form of seismic waves. These waves of energy ripple out in all directions from the point deep in Earth's crust where the breaking rock triggered an earthquake. This point is called the focus. From the focus, seismic waves travel through Earth's interior and up to the surface.

Inside an Earthquake

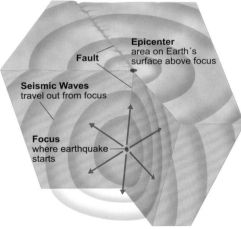

Epicenter
area on Earth's
surface above focus

Fault

Seismic Waves
travel out from focus

Focus
where earthquake
starts

▲ During an earthquake, seismic waves travel out in all directions from deep below the surface.

The epicenter is the location on the surface that sits directly above the focus. The energy from the seismic waves is greatest at the epicenter, but it may not be the point of the worst shaking. The amount and type of movement depend greatly on the type of seismic wave.

Types of Seismic Waves

There are two main types of seismic waves created during an earthquake. P, or primary, waves are the first to arrive. They are also the fastest. The vibrations from P waves push and pull at soil and rock. P waves can also pass through water and Earth's molten layers.

S, or secondary, waves follow the P waves. S waves are slower and can move only through solid rock. S waves move rock up and down or side to side, shaking the ground back and forth. When P or S waves reach the surface, they often transform into different types of surface waves. Like the P and S waves themselves, certain surface waves move the ground from side to side. Other types make the ground move as a wave moves across the ocean. Surface waves do not move as quickly as P waves and S waves, but they cause the biggest ground movement.

The seismic waves create vibrations that loosen dirt and rock. This is what

Seismographs

The type and frequency of seismic waves are two factors that affect how severe an earthquake may be. It is important for geologists to be able to measure the vibrations caused by these waves. A seismograph is an instrument that records ground movements during an earthquake. The jagged lines created by a seismograph represent the seismic waves. The greater the height of the spikes in the jagged lines, the stronger the earthquake.

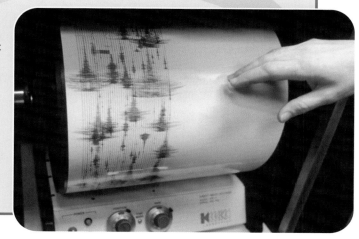

▶ The series of wide, jagged lines on this seismograph represents the activity of a very strong earthquake.

Catastrophe in Pakistan

On October 8, 2005, Pakistan was rocked by the most fatal earthquake in its history. Measuring 7.6 on the moment magnitude scale, the Pakistan earthquake took more than 73,000 lives and left nearly 3 million people homeless. The quake occurred in the area of a plate boundary that has experienced many earthquakes over the centuries. Historical documents show evidence of dramatic earthquakes in the Himalayas. Scientists believe that the 2005 earthquake, however, was the most violent in the region since the year 1555. As destructive as this earthquake was, scientists estimate that it unleashed only one-tenth of the energy that has built up along the faults in the region since the 1555 earthquake.

causes the shaking associated with earthquakes. If there is a limited amount of friction, the shaking may be no more than a mild rumbling under your feet. If the friction is great, however, the soil, rocks, and everything on them shake. In a city, this type of shaking may be strong enough to bring down buildings, roadways, and bridges.

Measuring Earthquakes

Over centuries, scientists have taken many factors into consideration when evaluating or measuring earthquakes.

Some factors relate to the amount of damage an earthquake causes. Others are based on intensity, or the amount of ground motion that takes place in a particular location during an earthquake.

In the early years of the twentieth century, geologists used the Mercalli scale, which rated an earthquake's intensity on a scale of 1 to 12. The scale was not a precise measurement, because it relied on a person's particular view of the effects of an earthquake. For example, an earthquake that caused people to run outdoors and created moderate to heavy damage was given a rating of 7 to 8 on the Mercalli scale. The definition of "moderate to heavy," however, might differ from one observer to the next.

Today, geologists who study earthquakes rely on specific measurements of seismic waves and the amount and type of movement along faults. These measurements show the magnitude, or strength, of an earthquake.

From the 1930s through the 1980s, geologists used the Richter scale to measure magnitude. This scale rates the size of seismic waves measured on a specific

▼ The March 1964 Alaska earthquake dropped this street in Anchorage 20 feet (6 m) below its normal level. The death toll of 115 people would have been much higher if the earthquake had taken place in a more populated area.

type of mechanical seismograph. The Richter scale worked well for smaller earthquakes that took place short distances away, but it was not very accurate for more distant earthquakes.

Geologists no longer have problems recording earthquakes at any point on the globe. Although we still hear about earthquakes being measured with the Richter scale, today's geologists use electronic seismographs and the moment magnitude scale. These measurements are used to rate all types of earthquakes, regardless of where they occur.

The first step in rating an earthquake using the moment magnitude scale is to take a close look at the data from a modern electronic seismograph. This information tells geologists the type and strength of the seismic waves the earthquake produced. The electronic data also indicates the amount of movement that took place along the fault, as well as how strong the rocks were that broke during the fault slip.

The moment magnitude scale rates earthquakes on a scale of about 3 to 10. An earthquake that measures less than 3.5 is so mild that it causes little or no damage. A few points higher, however, and it is a whole different story. An earthquake with a moment magnitude of 6.0 is almost 1,000 times as violent as one rated 4.0. A rating of 6.0 describes an earthquake that is capable of causing severe damage. With this as a guideline, try to imagine an earthquake that measured 9.2! This rating was given to the Great Alaska Earthquake of 1964, the most powerful earthquake ever recorded on U.S. soil.

▼ The fires caused by the 1906 San Francisco earthquake burned for four days. The damage left nearly half the city's population homeless.

Perhaps the most famous earthquake in U.S. history was the one that destroyed San Francisco in 1906. The combined effects of quake damage and the fires that broke out afterward leveled almost the entire city. Most of the fires were caused by broken gas mains. Because water mains were also broken, the fire brigades were unable to keep the fires from spreading. In the end, fire caused 90 percent of the total damage to the city.

Earthquakes are not just a danger to people living in places where there are tall buildings and modern streets. The violent shaking caused by seismic waves can result in avalanches or landslides that can carry away entire villages. Severe shaking can suddenly turn loose, moist soil into liquid mud. Any type of dwelling on top of this mud or in its path might sink, be pulled apart, or be buried.

Underwater Earthquakes

In December 2004, an earthquake rated 9.3 on the moment magnitude scale took place deep in the Indian Ocean. It was the second largest earthquake in

▲ Earthquakes sometimes cause mud slides that can carry away cars and parts of buildings.

recorded history. The earthquake caused a tsunami that resulted in horrifying death and destruction.

A tsunami occurs when an underwater earthquake causes the seafloor to rise or drop. This movement pushes water out of the way and forms waves. In the open sea, the waves are not very tall—maybe only about 3 feet (1 m) above the surface. As they get closer to shore, however, the waves increase in height and frequency.

In the 2004 Indian Ocean earthquake, some parts of the ocean floor suddenly rose as much as 16 feet (5 m). This type of jolt released a massive amount of energy— about as much energy as the United States uses in six months! That energy surge created waves that raced away from

the center of the earthquake at speeds of more than 500 miles (800 km) per hour. The first waves reached the island of Sumatra in Indonesia just fifteen minutes after the earthquake began. Waves almost 50 feet (15 m) tall slammed into the shore, sweeping everything from their path. Dwellings were flattened, and trees were tossed around like toothpicks.

Over the next few hours, the tsunami crashed into other nations in the region, including Thailand, Sri Lanka, and parts of India. The effects of this tsunami were felt as far away as the coast of South Africa, 5,000 miles (8,000 km) from the epicenter of the underwater earthquake.

The 2004 tsunami left more than 283,000 people either missing or dead—one of the highest-known death tolls resulting from a natural disaster. The destruction was terrible, but the under-sea earthquake had a more permanent impact. Earth now rotates about 2.67 milliseconds faster than it did before.

Although the 2004 tsunami made headlines around the world, many people still confuse tsunamis and tidal waves. Tidal waves are exactly what they are named for. They form from the action of tides. Tsunamis result specifically from underwater earthquakes, landslides, or volcanic eruptions.

Tsunami Warning System

After the 2004 tsunami, countries around the Indian Ocean teamed up to create a tsunami warning system. The system is similar to the one that was already in use by nations in the Pacific. The Pacific Tsunami Warning System relies on twenty-six member countries to evaluate earthquakes or other disturbances in the Pacific that may result in a tsunami. Sea-based seismic instruments can record an earthquake or volcanic activity taking place deep in the ocean. Since relatively few earthquakes actually result in a tsunami, other types of instruments are also needed. These include buoys that monitor activity on the ocean's surface. The buoys gather information about the size and frequency of waves traveling across the water. They transmit that information to satellites in orbit around Earth. The satellites then communicate the information to a tsunami warning center. These centers, such as the one close to Honolulu, Hawaii, can warn authorities if a tsunami is about to strike.

▶ Banda Aceh, the capital city of Aceh province in Indonesia, was one of the areas hardest hit by the December 2004 tsunami.

7 VOLCANOES

A volcano is one of the most stunning examples of the link between Earth's core and crust. Volcanoes form at weak spots in Earth's crust where hot mantle material, or magma, rises toward the surface. Magma is a combination of gases, water, and molten rock. Magma that reaches the surface is called lava. As it cools, lava eventually hardens and becomes solid rock.

Hot Rock and Gases

Often when people think about volcanoes, an image comes to mind of a huge mountain spitting fire and thick smoke into the sky. To be sure, throughout history, such volcanic activity has deposited layer upon layer of cooled lava rock on the surface. All these layers create landforms on Earth's surface, as well as many of the world's islands. Not all volcanoes erupt with such fury, however. Sometimes an eruption includes far less fire and color and much more bubbling hot rock. Whatever form an eruption takes, though, the factors that cause eruptions remain the same.

▲ The volcano Kilauea in Hawaii has been constantly erupting since 1983. Its lava flows travel slowly over land and often reach the ocean.

Magma is a liquid that is less dense than some of the heavier mantle material. It rises to the top of the asthenosphere, where it is trapped beneath the rockier part of the upper lithosphere. This hot material, with its dissolved gases, is under a great deal of pressure. What do you think is likely to happen?

Almost everyone has dropped an unopened can of soda. If you were unlucky enough to try to immediately open the can, you probably got wet when the soda shot out of the small opening. Soda contains carbon dioxide gas that forms bubbles. The soda in the can is already under pressure. When you open the can, the bubbles that have collected at the surface shoot out and bring the soda with them. Something similar happens with the gases in magma.

As the magma rises, the dissolved gases begin to separate out and form at the top of the magma. When a volcano erupts, it is like the can being opened. The bubbles rush out, pulling the magma with them. How quickly the bubbles and magma rush out depends on several factors. The temperature and thickness of the magma, the amount of dissolved gases, and the amount of a specific material called silica affect how explosive a volcanic eruption will be.

Vulcan's Forge

The ancient Romans believed that volcanoes erupted when Vulcan, their god of fire, got his forge ready to make armor and weapons for the other gods. Because the gods disagreed frequently, Vulcan kept busy. His forge was thought to be located beneath Mount Etna on the island of Sicily in Italy.

Mount Etna is one of the world's largest and most active volcanoes. Geologists believe that some of its earliest eruptions occurred about 300,000 years ago. Experts also believe that Etna was once an underwater volcano. Mount Etna's first recorded eruption was in 1500 B.C. Since then, it has erupted at least 191 times.

In most cases, the hotter the magma, the thinner, or more fluid, it is. A thinner fluid with a high amount of dissolved gases and low silica content is more likely to quietly bubble out of small cracks or other openings in the volcano. Thick, silica-rich magma moves more slowly. Trapped gases develop more pressure and push on the magma. The increased pressure in combination with the thick magma often results in violent and spectacular eruptions.

Volcanoes can be active, dormant, or extinct. An active volcano is one that is

Inside a Volcano

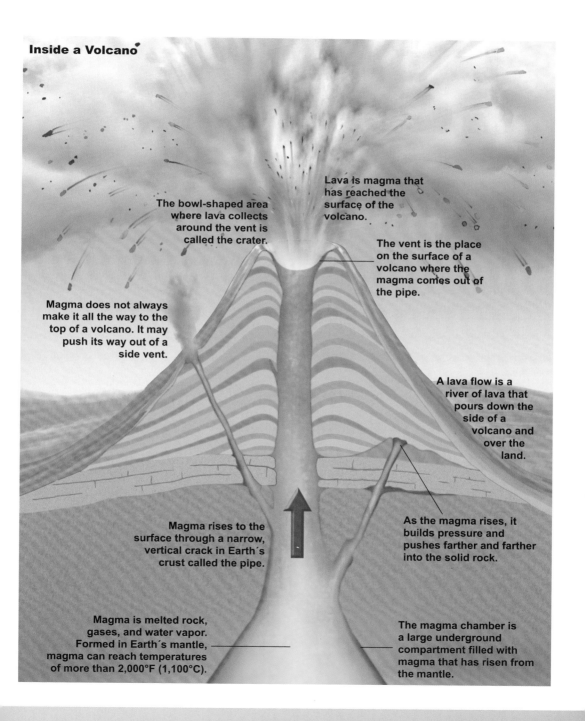

The bowl-shaped area where lava collects around the vent is called the crater.

Lava is magma that has reached the surface of the volcano.

The vent is the place on the surface of a volcano where the magma comes out of the pipe.

Magma does not always make it all the way to the top of a volcano. It may push its way out of a side vent.

A lava flow is a river of lava that pours down the side of a volcano and over the land.

Magma rises to the surface through a narrow, vertical crack in Earth's crust called the pipe.

As the magma rises, it builds pressure and pushes farther and farther into the solid rock.

Magma is melted rock, gases, and water vapor. Formed in Earth's mantle, magma can reach temperatures of more than 2,000°F (1,100°C).

The magma chamber is a large underground compartment filled with magma that has risen from the mantle.

▲ The mushroom-shaped plume from the May 1980 Mount St. Helens eruption rose 12 miles (19 km) into the sky.

erupting or showing signs that it might erupt sometime soon. In Washington State in 1980, geologists saw smoke and small eruptions on Mount St. Helens for two months before a huge eruption tore off the top of the volcano.

A dormant, or sleeping, volcano is expected to erupt again in the future. In other words, a dormant volcano has the elements of an active volcano, but nothing is happening. Extinct volcanoes show no activity. They are not expected to erupt ever again.

Frozen in Time

In 79 A.D., Mount Vesuvius in Italy was the site of one of the most explosive volcanic eruptions in history. Burning ash, poisonous gases, and fire swept through Pompeii, an ancient Roman resort town located in the shadow of the mountain. When magma blasts into the air, it breaks apart into fragments called tephra. Tephra can be the size of boulders or as fine as powder. In Pompeii, fleeing citizens were covered by a 10-foot (3-m) layer of tephra. In 1860, excavations of the site revealed oddly shaped spaces in the hardened ash. Archaeologists made plaster casts of the spaces. The casts revealed that the spaces were actually the outlines of people and animals (such as the dog below) that had been trapped. Most died immediately from the poison gases that flowed from the erupting volcano. Hot ash fell on their bodies and hardened when rains came the following day. The bodies decayed, but the shapes remained. Today, the casts are fascinating examples of the destructive capabilities of volcanoes.

All Over the World

Volcanoes exist all over Earth. About 600 active volcanoes are found on land. Some scientists estimate that there are thousands of active volcanoes under the ocean's waters. Many volcanoes are found along divergent boundaries—between plates that are moving away from each other. The mid-ocean ridge is a common location for volcanoes. After all, the mid-

The Ring of Fire

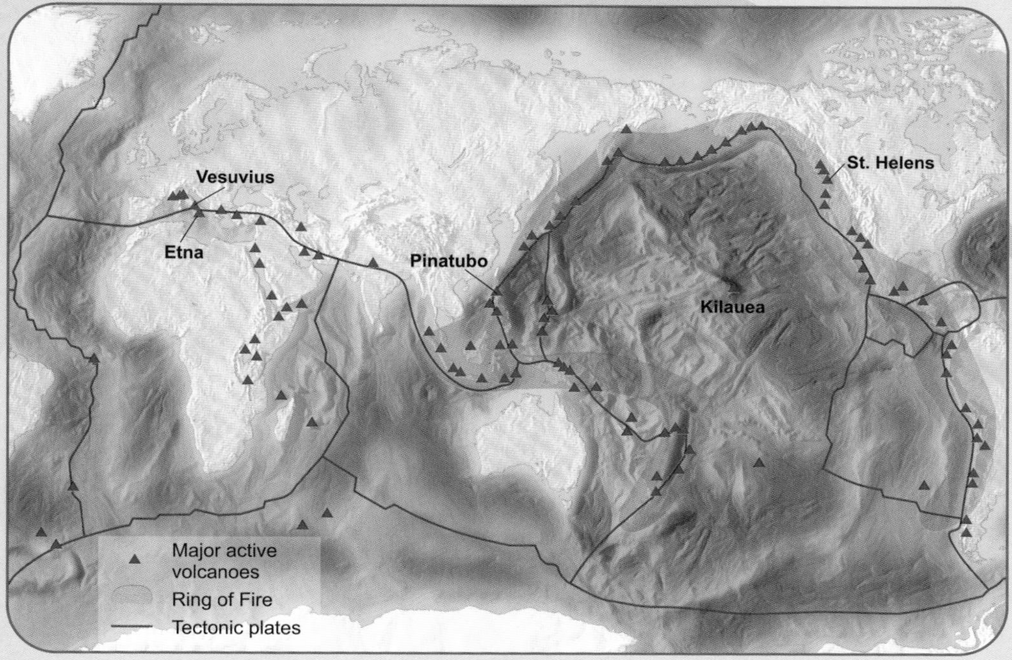

Vesuvius

Etna

Pinatubo

Kilauea

St. Helens

▲ Major active volcanoes

Ring of Fire

— Tectonic plates

A belt of volcanoes almost 25,000 miles (40,000 km) long rims the Pacific Ocean. More than 75 percent of Earth's active and dormant volcanoes are located here. This group of volcanoes is called the Pacific Ring of Fire. The Ring of Fire follows the borders of major tectonic plates. One of these plates, the Pacific Plate, runs along the west coast of the United States. Earthquakes and volcanic eruptions are frequent along the ring. In fact, more than 80 percent of the most severe earthquakes on Earth occur in the Ring of Fire. Four out of five tsunamis also take place within this very active area.

ocean ridge is formed of mantle material that has seeped through the oceanic crust. You would expect to find volcanoes in those areas. Some of the volcanoes of the mid-ocean ridge rise above the surface of the ocean. The island of Iceland is an examples of this.

Volcanoes are also common near the deep-ocean trenches that form at convergent boundaries. The oceanic crust subducts through the trench and drops back down into Earth's mantle. When the magma comes up through the oceanic crust, it creates volcanoes. Subduction at convergent plates created most of the volcanoes that form the Pacific Ring of Fire.

There are spots on Earth's crust where the magma is hot enough and the crust weak enough that the magma acts like a blowtorch heating up a relatively small area of crust. These areas are called hot spots. Often, hot spots are found far from plate boundaries. The Hawaiian Islands and Yellowstone National Park in Wyoming are two well-known hot spots.

▲ Iceland is located over a volcanic hot spot. It is also part of the Mid-Atlantic Ridge. These two factors combine to make Iceland a place of especially active volcanoes. One of them, Laki (above), produced the greatest amount of lava for any volcano in recorded history.

8 EARTH'S CORE AND CRUST

Sometimes it is hard to imagine that the rocks and soil beneath your feet are part of an active system. It is hard to fathom that a revolving ball of magnetic iron thousands of miles below, at the center of Earth, has anything to do with your day-to-day life.

The fact remains, though, that Earth's core and crust are just as much a part of your daily life as the air you breathe and the food you eat. The interactions between Earth's layers have formed the ground on which you stand, the lakes and oceans in which you swim, and the caves, canyons, and mountains you may explore in your lifetime.

There is still a great deal to learn about Earth's core and crust. Finding ways to gain that knowledge is a challenge itself. Perhaps one day you will be the scientist who discovers how to probe deeper toward Earth's core.

▼ Yellowstone National Park, one of nature's hot spots, is home to some of the most amazing geothermal activity in the world. Its natural attractions include geothermal terraces *(top right)*, colorful geothermal pools *(bottom right)*, and the legendary geyser Old Faithful *(left)*.

GLOSSARY

asthenosphere The soft layer of the mantle, located just below the more rigid lithosphere

basalt A volcanic lava rock that is denser than granite

continental crust The surface that lies under continents and all large landmasses; it contains all major landforms, such as mountains, canyons, and caves

continental drift A theory of Alfred Wegener's that all the continents once formed a great landmass but moved apart over millions of years

convection A process in which heat is transferred by the movement of matter from one place to another

convection current The flow of warmer liquid rising and cooler liquid falling that transfers heat in a liquid

convergent boundary A place where two plates come together

core The hot, solid center of Earth

crust The solid surface of Earth consisting of landforms, such as mountains, valleys, caves, and the ocean floor

divergent boundary A border between two plates that are moving away from each other

earthquake A shaking or trembling of earth caused by a volcanic eruption or plate movements; a sudden movement of rock along a fault

epicenter The point on the surface directly above the focus of an earthquake

fault A break in Earth's surface where huge blocks or slabs of rock slide past each other

fault zone A series of faults that extends for many miles on Earth's surface

focus The point where rock breaks and an earthquake occurs

fossil A remnant, a bone, or trace of an animal or plant that died long ago

geologist A scientist who studies Earth and its history

geosphere The layer of Earth that contains all the solid surfaces, mountains, lowlands, and the ocean floor

inner core The dense, solid metal center of Earth; it consists mostly of iron and nickel

lava Molten rock from a volcano or a break in Earth's surface that becomes hard rock when it cools

lithosphere The crust and the solid uppermost part of the mantle

mantle A thick main layer of Earth that lies between the crust and the outer core; it is about 1,800 miles (2,900 km) deep and consists mostly of oxygen, iron, silicon, and magnesium

mid-ocean ridge A chain of mountains encircling Earth for more than 40,000 miles (64,000 km) on the ocean floor

oceanic crust The part of the crust that forms the ocean floor; it is made mostly of volcanic rock

outer core A liquid layer of hot molten rock that lies between the mantle and the inner core; it is about 1,400 miles (2,250 km) thick and consists of molten iron and nickel

plate tectonics A theory that Earth's continental and oceanic crusts consist of large landmasses, or plates, whose movement creates valleys, mountains, deep-ocean trenches, earthquakes, and volcanoes

rift valley A long, large depression in Earth caused when two plates pull apart at a divergent boundary

seafloor spreading The process of hot mantle material pushing up through the crust and causing a ridge to expand on either side

seismic wave Energy that ripples out from the focus of an earthquake

subduction A process in which a section of one plate moves beneath another and into the mantle

subduction zone An area where an oceanic plate meets a continental plate and sinks below it and into the mantle

transform boundary A place where two plates slide past each other

volcano An opening in Earth's crust where magma comes to the surface

FURTHER INFORMATION

Books
Moores, Eldridge M. (ed.). *Volcanoes and Earthquakes.* New York: Barnes and Noble Books, 2003.

Stille, Darlene R. *Plate Tectonics: Earth's Moving Crust.* Minneapolis: Compass Point Books, 2007.

Thompson, Luke. *Tsunamis.* New York: Scholastic Books, 2000.

Web Sites
Extreme 2002: Mission Into the Abyss
www.ocean.udel.edu/extreme2002

Forces of Nature
www.nationalgeographic.com/forcesofnature

On the Move ... Continental Drift and Plate Tectonics
kids.earth.nasa.gov/archive/pangaea/index.html

Savage Earth: Waves of Destruction: Tsunamis
www.pbs.org/wnet/savageearth/animations/tsunami/index.html

U.S. Geological Survey Earthquake Hazards Program: Latest Earthquakes
earthquake.usgs.gov/eqcenter

DVDs
Forces of Nature. National Geographic, 2004.

Living Rock: Earth's Geology. U.S. Geological Survey and Alpha, 2002.

INDEX

3 2186 00163 9391

Fossil Ridge Public Library District
Braidwood, IL 60408